Bridge between Temple and Dream

Poems from Lonely Nature

Jennifer Darland

Arts of Earth and Sky

Copyright © 2025 by Jennifer Darland

Arts of Earth and Sky

All rights reserved. No part of this book may be reproduced or transmitted in any form or by any means, electronic or mechanical, including photocopying, recording, scanning, posting to a website, or by any information storage and retrieval system, without permission in writing from the publisher.

ISBN: 979-8-9995355-1-1

Bridge between Temple and Dream: Poems from Lonely Nature

Arts of Earth and Sky

All text and cover art is original work by Jennifer Darland

To Valerie

Also by Jennifer Darland

The Answer Wheel:
360 Illuminations for the Human Spirit

Jennifer's Travels:
Moonscapes of Recombobulation

Bridge between Temple and Dream

Contents

1. Lucidity 1
2. Canyon Ceremony 4
3. Flux On 7
4. Deliverance 13
5. I'm Hers 17
6. She Demon 19
7. Dance with the Departed 22
8. A Message through the Far Sky 25
9. After Seeing the Sea 27
10. The Future 33
11. Eyes 35
12. That Which Never Dies 38
13. Tomorrow's Fallen Ashes 41
14. Breaking off a Tough Piece 43
15. A Glimpse of Boundless Heart 46
16. Taste of Pacing 48
17. I Wear Her 50
18. The Inversion of Winter's Noon 53
19. Sun Seduction 58
20. Night Stallions 61
21. The Feminine Ignited 65
22. Clarity 69
23. Space for a Breath 73
24. Charm 76
25. One 79

Lucidity

Naked, lucidity tonight

The burn of freedom smolders through the smoky skies

Nocturnal yearning, she slips out from her skin

Seduces the air, flirting with dimensions

And I smell her, as she falls into my bed

    Echoes of the stream flow through her whispers

    Diamonds streak the hillside where her body lay

Darkened timbers, she travels with the oak

Alder blossoms woven through her hair and mine

Scent of palm fruit, sticky down her thighs

As the forest hides the sky all around me

She rides in by the wings of tonight

Through the shake of windy leaves, she brings the moonlight

The nymph running wild inside my mind

She warms me with her breath where my body lies

And we embrace the legends of the night

Tender mystery,

    I hold the moonbeam tight

Ripples of pleasure's shadows shiver through my skin

I swallow ashes to find out what time I'm in

A puff of smoke

The nighttime broke

And I'm still faraway

The sheath of misty darkness kissed me goodbye again

Then, the morning birds paint the sky blue

The quiver in my fingertip reaches for you

And the crystal morning star shines her grace into my heart

Naked sunrise

On another lucid flight.

Canyon Ceremony

Feathertip kiss of the wind on my lip

A brush of fragrant everlasting moves me

Waterfalls sound the way

    Paths drawn by footprints of beasts

        A passage through time

Histories of stones fixed by boulders of eras

Quartz mosaics converse with ancient stars

    Bantering with light from eons ago

Oak wooden dragons, more alive than most men

    Cosmic Mother, come touch me.

The mantle finds a beat

    As the earth below rumbles

    Spirit treads through my steps

A red tail hawk my escort,
the bobcat spies

The sun is too bright, but I
love facing east

Caressed by lupine, sage soaks the space

Gateway between temple and dream

Threads of taproots in a messy bunch,

Earth's tangled hair combed by the
stream's path

Rocks glisten

Iron and copper paradise islands

Pink granite skips

To the waterfall's tune

As it races the frolicking butterflies
down the stream

There is no such ceremony as this

Hatched fairies racing out, eager to live

The sun strikes their faces

And reflects glittering joy upon mine

Rainbow wings

    Most suitable blessings for such a day

        Where the canyon calls me home

            Secluded in its jagged walls.

Flux On

1.

Fountains of life bubble within,
consciousness cascading

Landscapes of self, pressures are changing

The abrasions of the frenzied masses
sculpt the war drum skins upon my heart

Shields and armor spring from worry,
heroes tour my mind

As I float within the harbors of my
destiny.

Cards flash divinations,

    revealing answers since I'd
bothered to ask

    The hierophant teaches and the
priestess prevails

        Masquerading as the
    masters of my mind

Entities that inhabit me one after one.

The lens discerns and the vision of art saves me

        Memories colored by the gift of transcendence

        The victim anew once slashed to pieces

    Upon the rubble, relief splashes

An ounce of humidity settles on the smoky haze

    and then I'm drenched

        as clouds burst open and thunder cracks in my veins

        Clenched fists washed away in the deluge

        of realization

        Unique to this moment

        Becoming

            someone

                again.

2.

     Ditch the umbrella and relish in the rain, she told me.

That friend who looks the same as me and I kissed her everywhere

As we stood there in the pouring rain

     That night on Friendship Street.

         When my insides hollowed and I let her in,

Pink plumes billowing out into the universe

     And we cried smiling

The remnants of what we once were.

A vessel filled thick with memory, contained in an endless mist

     That nurtures fields of flowers

Every time we choose to feel it.

And we laughed in faces and words, saying,

     Maybe we must just take our turns

> For a brief incarnation as a beetle,
>
> Hard, cold, and unloved
>
> Squished by shoes and tissues.

But that was in the past,

And now it's now, not quite gone yet.

3.

So I breathe slowly, embrace the garden and the bounty of life

> As golden devas leap into the air
>
> Goddesses born of stamens lashing out in joy
>
> > Lavish silken petal dresses
>
> Undulating with the sunshine, spreading open for rain

And my cat's slick hair glimmers in the sun

His rough tongue scraping my palm as he purrs his own story

> > Now that's life

   As my sensitive skin
forgives the passion of his kneading claws

  Sharpened by the elder oaks

The gentle punctures are my own love
speaking back, in gesture.

4.

The reverberation of endless impulses
rotate through our experience

   The orchestration of the bow that
strikes the infinite

     That bends through space
  and finds shape in water

      And secures homes
in our thoughts and actions,

Living on through our perception

  The culmination of all intent
perpetually grinding,

    communal tension

     and release.

The grand mass of intuition,

    Chatterings in fluctuation,

        Eternity always shifting.

Deliverance

Risen by the universe again, the essence of mystery beholds me

The venom of the spider brooding in my veins

The shine of falling stars yields to the sunlight

    Eternal darkness is looming beyond light blues

        The illusion that spares us from forever

            The sun scribes riddles told in phases

    And I watch heaven through the rays of the daytime

        Where the bodies of night won't show to anyone

But I rise through the fog, consciousness sifted

> Starlights are falling behind the veil of light
>> Where spindles of dreams are wound and folded
>> Bounties of stardust spiral through the night
>> Dreamboats surfing shadows and I'm gliding
>> Flung for miles over deep indigos of skies

The brightness of tonight climbs over meteors

Perfecting purple tones that rescue souls

While unlocking the tarnished doors of insight

Saying symbols are the keys to our salvation

Inky maps disperse our shadows and form destinies

Winding into paths that pave our stories

Glistening through wonders of the sky

Rivers of myths endlessly flowing

    Show me now my meaning lies in sleep

The blacks and whites of gods shimmer as I fall

The strobes are hints of faces and flickering

    Through droplets over spotlights in the city.

And I land in the valley where my heart is born

    The soil is soft and it's fertile there

    The grassy lands of promises and healing

And then the sticky hold of night dispels me

I plunge through nodes of silence and it's noisy there

From the treetops I tumble down

        flights of leaves

And through the secrets of my slumber,
meanings are shifting

      Time lets go, and dresses me in
pure white wings

      And I leave my body on the soil to
marry with the light

            I weigh nothing
         while a blissful sound
         envelops me

      And I'm cast into the stars,
cold and falling

I shiver once

      and look, the sky is black now.

I'm Hers

The forest of the angels sings the mountains to sleep

Through crickets and katydids

    Rounds of duets, batons of harmonies passed

    From the frogs to the mating cats

A rain of flowers invokes a celestial dance,

Chanting for the clouds to pour

    Maracas rattle in the branches, spirits speak inside wind

        The invisible quest

    Where immortals whisper truth

        To those who will listen

Dragon my beloved host, I wander in my formless ghost

    Settled on a dream of green,

        Trichomes from the plants

Doves are sleeping, hearts turn wild,

        Escape the chase of the haunted night raven

My little child takes a ride in the wind and runs free in the sky

        Frames of time propel her

The goddess churns her mill, the mystery

        Night time moans, spirits flee

                Voyage of stillness, the tide to forever

Deer parade, the carnivores hide

Glowing eyes on boats of leaves

This piece of time is where she can find me,

        Let nature guide me,

                I'm Hers.

She Demon

She must be a demon, that woman in black

Hovering over the white snow, nothing else moving

Frozen in time, staring through the cold eye of the needle

That knits future with past.

Time is torn as wolves nip at the bottom of her tattered dress

Until they expire, buried in snow

Nothing else moving, she is still

In the white desert drift.

Her skin fades in and out of the fabric of the day

She comes and disappears

She cuts through forbidden air

Emerging unscathed, in chiseled perfection.

Ice sculpture secret sneaking towards me

She withdraws into her cold hard hood, all black

Teasing shadows with her carved cheekbones

The edges of her eyes slice barriers

Sharp as knives that cut the world away

Red foggy breath spills from her tongue

As her laugh recoils down my spine

In accord with the crimson flash in her eyes.

The snowflakes trace our chamber of solitude, our eyes are fastened

We barter for our fallen fragments, exchange parts for each other

As lights bounce off the cold hard white

And go anywhere but her.

A sliver of time yet forever in her face
Released from her cloak at the sweep of my hand
Cinnamon dreams infused with whiskey
And I find myself shaking
In the cedar grove at dawn, hungry at the edge of town
As she is ripped away by the wretched morning rainbows
An invasion to the domination of her eyes
And the death in her ravenous smile.

The animated dead are lurking in the mud
Rising from the melted snow
I'm captive in stillness,
My frost-nipped toes howling.

Dance with the Departed

A stomp into the ash, arrival into the unknown

Fire roars through silent tunnels, the thunderous echo of what has passed

Burned slopes cut into the skyline, naked and sucked dry

Wildlands dusted down to a grey silt

I stroll through warm smoky powders, lost in landmarks of destruction

Where noble trees once strong
are broken

With their comrades, charred and fallen

Graveyards of ghosts lead to the leg of a doe

    Where footsteps fall quiet

And skeleton trees stand testimony,

    A reminder that nature rules.

Hopping cracked stones along spreads of cinders

      Strewn with charcoal and bone

A glimpse into the afterlife

A peek through wooden shards in fields of daggers

      Where the rapture of the dead will seize you

      Where intact skulls carry on in underworld festivals,

            Bridging banquets of
            flesh and dream

      And I dance with the departed.

Fresh whirling spirits diffuse as chalky air, essence of oak streams by

Peace of the deer waves through like a ribbon, life appears from millennia ago.

         The bones of his fingers,
         I take death's hand

     as he blows a glowing ember and welcomes me in

A brittle caution runs dry in the rock's veins

And death gathers in the brightest place

  as he leans in for a kiss

    On the verge of twilight

    I see the spark and remember to feel

    Then he crumbles to ash,

      and I am alive.

A Message through the Far Sky

I blow the feather to your front door

Meanwhile, you are sleeping

The arc of the moon curves over your bed

And you awaken from the backs of your eyes

A star falls and offers to trade for the night

She needs a rest

You rise and move mountains

To jump time

You tumble through rivers, limbless

To see me

Burning, in the cool relief of the night.

The owl watches, perched on the tree

Changes wisdom for sonar from the bats

The atmosphere pulses, her message flies

To her sisters and brothers

And to the wise
grandmother owl

Whose feather blew away
last night

Guard the mystic of the land

Descendent of the sky

For tomorrow she will celebrate all life

And your feather

Is at my door

After Seeing the Sea

The cliffs at the top of the sands wake me

Decibels louder each hour of night

My senses leak into their spells

And their calling seeps into my dreams

    The longing for knowledge pulls me

    Sleepwalking and eyes crazed

        Traffic lights do not find me

        No eyes pass by me as I stride along

        Hypnotic towards the shoreline

        Untouched by anything

A thin rail of cliff points to an island

    And I dive into the torrent of rocky sea

       The power of the gods
wielded in the waves

            Crashing like thunderbolts
right beside me

                  Giants in salty waters
          command this world womb

              Tridents and
hurricanes raging beneath

         Storms of life and death are
secretly stirring

             Conspiring,
considering my doom

I reach the tiny island, circled in by both arms

                  A vapor breath, a
                  taste of God, it's
                  riveting

         With all my might, on
heaven's chains, I step up there

            I push my chest into
rampant flumes, strangely settling

The wind whips me now and it's cold, but I'm still standing

Thrashing waves are hurled at me, and I'm stiffening

                The hand of God,
           some buoyancy, encases me

Consciousness from continents sent in weathervanes

The pain of the world spits needles at my skin

Encircled in tight bangs of freezing waters

         Slapping at my feet, both
         firm but shaking

    Each joint of my toes grips to the stony mound

         A jolt of life shoots up
     through me from underneath

         From the trickster of
         this island that has forsaken
         me

The seastorm laughs, dares me to sing my victory

The eyes upon my chest steer me to the sky

    I find my compass there, my starboard, my sacred soul

        I smile overhead, stuck here, and frozen now

        Hardened up and too shut down for feeling.

    My reserve of air from deep within comes flooding

        Ringing glory while my voice is carried by gods on high

    The freedom in my battle cry soothes the tempest at sea

        Warrior sirens form my chorus in the distance

United spirit, I'm humbled down and safe now here

There's lightning twice and then a boat comes sailing in

    It's empty and the waves are smooth in World Mother's womb

    Sparkling mystic fins reflect the early light

        The first to ever see me,
        and then they swim away.

The sailboat rocks when sea gulls land to host the sunrise

    I wade through calm waters to the morning beach

        Where sunshine falls
      sweetly on the sprays

A little child belly laughing wobbles on the shore

Her tiny feet run freely towards the water

I wash ashore into a cave inside tall tight cliffs

    I press my head onto the sand

    Where the lull of the stable earth sends me to sleep for days

        Never the same

            After seeing the sea.

The Future

Any day now,
The jubilant heart of the mountains
Will bulge through the veins of the globe
Unbearable manmade ruins
Will fall through cracks of time
The pendulum shall draw a new arc,
A blooming abode
Where all thrive
Families cast in bronze will shine,
The prize is within
Love flourishes
Debris of the ocean self-devours
The sea renews with life
Booming on salty cliffs
Pollution exhausts itself
And hands the space to fragrant air

Soaked with nature's scent

The forest, the worker's ally

Our roots shall intertwine

Animals prosper, mutual citizens

The current of the waters

Makes love to the sky's turn

And baby's breath

Makes new again

Eyes

Those spokes in your eyes are spiraling

        Luring me in

Mossed glass and bark or hazel blues

The wheels of possibility turning

        Driving their way into my
        inclinations

We are all too broken to stare, locked out of our own truth

        But instead we imagine

Beyond pine's passage, past the sight of perception

From the corners of the atmosphere, a vision bestows us

        Propelling us away from the weary heap of common lethargy.

        We all say the same thing, tired.

        But not those eyes.

   A collage of freedom, wet with elixir

  Kaleidoscope treasures that revolve latent doorways

Clasps of rusty dungeons rupture

   Lost faces make their marks on stone cathedrals

Allowing us inside the refuge of the gods

   Totems stacked with stories, enchantments the heights of trees

   Folded in the mountains, blanketed by the stars,

     Where a portal opens up

     And introduces us to ourselves.

We gaze to the galaxy and search for our fates

     Relays of the planets, the songs of the spheres mingle

A ballet of episodes spins through the sky

   As we taste of potions and wine

Venus moves to dawn,

        A fractal to gift a crystal morning

The horns of Isis guard the night,

        On tiptoes she is glorified

        She elegantly moves to the center of the stage

Where the man with the silver sword

            Washed clean by the rain

        Stands by

                And awaits her touch.

That Which Never Dies

Her eerie breath creeps along my neckline

She who blinks with rainbows and paints new eyes

    Recycles time

    Eternal witness

Chills spill over the breeze across my fingertips

Wrapped up in the swarm as bees fly around an unseasonably warm

    winter day in California

This will be the moon of alder blossoms

    chalky yellow dusted everything

Whistled winds whisper, some leaves spinning as they fall

    Vayus as whirling gods
scrub my skin

   And the foxes feed from
their mother all at once

    Little cones growing as the
young hawk calls

    A nest made with my hair
and the wren flies by

And the first primal sounds seed into my wholeness,

   receiving this

My eternal self of peace.

I take on the day, joyous in my womb, my tomb

   This vessel of immortal being

   Where I interact with changes, alchemical outcomes

Over eyes of potential Buddha smiles

    Stillness waiting for action.

 The pull of life praises rain and hope

      Creation, hosts of muses
      and animals grazing

    Conception, invoking promises
    with light and sound

        which manifest the colors

The eternal ether of ancient ways that

Whets the space for the flagrant juice of divine exchange

          Nectar of life, birth of soul,

Everlasting motion, nurturing decay,

Lifetime fed who summons the rains

Clouds breaking open with life

Cleansing what we've used

    Churning what's alive, passing it on

    This is that which never dies

    And to know that always

        Is to flow with time

Tomorrow's Fallen Ashes

Her fingers run through my hair in the morning

                Only her body is gone

A splash onto my palm lines, a deep story runs through me

Burning embers as treasures in my hand

                That touched

        Protected places where we are

Descendants of darkness in our sacred womb

Satin wings dancing in half-moon shadows

She moves and speaks like flowing ink painting words

Wolfen eyes that howl for the moon

        An invitation into midnight

And the sun disk gateway swirled inside clouds

       The chariot emerges wielding
       wands of wisdom over open skies

Where she travelled through time to keep
tomorrow coming

       When we crossed past the veil at
       the edge of night

         The secrets we dream
break free in our breath

On the candlelit bridge

       Her heart in my hand,

Beating wild as we shape this

       Goddess bears witness

Closer and closer and time stands still

         The world in this moment

               Kiss

Then the soft gown of dreaming

               slides
off my shoulders

       Tomorrow's Fallen Ashes

Breaking off a Tough Piece

Mounds of mangled tapestries unravel

Crusty blooded dust crystals disperse, shrieking in exile

A red vital river of oneness bursts through, perceptions paved

    Grit and stagnation blown away, softened faces

    The seer sees from vibrant eyes, clarity recovers

        As ten thousand ants
        crawling over my head
        die to five

The bows of masters stroke chords of muscle into feeling

Dissonance of broken structures finds me again on the way out

    They shake out into music

        Mud falls off swerving hips

     While I dance alone
     One with heart

To soak the sun inside crane white wings,
   Agni's fire bakes earthen roots
   Faces in broken windows
screaming over violin
   Memory strikes, tripled in mirrors
Their dying breath released as fog
   Shattering of past
   Agony dismantles, dissolution of
transitory fables

A single ray of sun magnifies quiet beams
   Rousing placid waters
     And humor lashes out from
ionic waves
   Temple bells in heavy metals
where I fly

        Lightning strikes and Shakti
merges with my watery seas

              By soma set sail

Falling free,

body empty and light

      I converge with the moon

      I am the force behind me

           She who makes thunder
with sound

      I am thee from which I came

           I carry nothing

A Glimpse of Boundless Heart

The shock of sudden awareness

Lanterns shine forward on the path

Radiating far out from the main drag

      An arc of space that parallels time forever blooming

         Spirals of infinity winding

Endless mazes of dizzy distractions, a fuzzy mess of constraint

      Is what we triumph with our boundless hearts

Illuminated and refined by challenge

Clear in what we want to see and creative if we believe it

As we spin our way through fleeting shinings,

      finding and losing our way again

It's the spark that drives us to be here

Just lifting our feet

                      And going that way

                              Expansion

We hold ourselves holy to find it

      Starlight within

      Source of light

              Our own unique place

              We can always return

May you be my guide as eternity's face

        The abode of my faithful refuge

The gods have roared for my release

        Jury of rulers in the skies

                And stars shoot fate arrows

                That can strike anything

Taste of Pacing

    We name it a rain of flowers, tender and wide

    Nature's call, we run blindly into the wilderness

        Your sleek body gleams, ropes of muscles shine brilliance in light

Aerodynamic for slipping through long braids of weeping trees

    I take a dip in a bead of your sweat

        Your mouth, thirsty for the ground's water

    Too primal for a cup, you sip

And then you drink from me

    We trip through the canopy and fuse into sky

We leap frog into future nights

Carried away by caws and quails and crickets

    In southern winter storms
of naked prowling

    Where ocean mist arrives
through old shells

    And serrated leaves damp
with mountain water

   And wild things cast living scents

As we tour sensations and then note,

What is that force that takes us there?

   Walk on, I hear her say

   The cosmic sunset is just ahead

     It's getting oranger,

   Take your time.

I Wear Her

The riches of woman's skin

Sweet fruit glaze on her apple heart face

Spills of thrills as I remember her smile

    The corners just a little shy

And she sends me what she's worn

Her scent and aspen, two hairs on the sleeve

    And inside the jeans

Ripped holed knees from her adventures

    Or did her artist cut them
    in play she adores

She undid these buttons, hung and folded

She sweat inside and shivered there

    I step into her embroidered denim

        She attends me on my walk

           Hands holding

Dexterous fingers fabricate dream

She laughs of puppies yelping everywhere

    Wild beast souls entering selves

Appetites grow into walking sleeps

The blackness of new moon hides her

        And we step in stride with the throes of the night

        Where quiet still lakes may let secrets rise free

            In midnight hazes

And reflective waters beyond the moon

        Darkened rainbows exchange

        Dressed in her threads,

        Tethered by mountain and tied on my shoulder

As we awake apart, continuums cast in smiles

    Joyous union

    Our daily patdowns of claws

    The life force of forest shooting up through our bare soles

The pattering of cloven hoofs

        Ripen ancient peace
        we witness

        May we alter evil

And I notice a new star under crisp bites

    of shiny red-appled air

Ceilings of skies dappled in wonders

Provoked by cycles of passionate night passing

Emptied by naked nature

    And then a shudder of loneliness

No faces

        Until there is you

    Dreaming under light blues again

The wet forest floor brings me home

    I slip the white lace off my neck,

        Your black dress
        that held us.

The Inversion of Winter's Noon

1.

High ten and dreamcast again

Displaced night journeys over

Rowing dark waters toward the distant
lands of day

Shapes inverting in the trees I know

      To be otherwise

           Gnarled masses of
branched hairs go berserk

      Hysteria buried by silence,
equilibrium striven I wade in the thick

Greyed eyes wishing me death
in glaring basins of black

Harsh stories of time lashing from
their rugged barks

           Shit and spits of it stained
           up and down my back

The vacancy of woman trips me flat again

Spoken in the stream, I'm told to hold onto

Those stray strips of hope

    And let them drive me

Ease squanders to a screeching halt

    Pestering the frayed nerves into a further frenzy

Silos of faces spinning, which one do I choose

    To embody or prey

Crowds of shadows blot out my face,

    Smeared perception, a calming dissolution

    Fragments of circuits breeding derangement, daytime expels me

Twisted snarls consume me and I succumb to black

    Snatched up by the shackles of night's needy tendrils

    Dark goddess having her feed

2.

                The creek is louder
         now, a pitch perfect D

Pains of silence whipped clean with new waters electric by clouds

Beauty flowered by sadness withering

The breech of the steel sky fading

Residue of harmonic disturbance, hovering pastel swirls in the sky

      Sunrays as seen by the edge of red's blade

      Dissecting my forked tongue hidden

The secrets of perpetual slicing, mechanism within

Underworld self, equal as me and sharper

Concentric ripples circle night's swamp, closing in, constriction of day

A force to devour my own deception

The betrayal of midnight's mirror, false beauty's fool

My face drowns away as she feeds of
flesh, corners of skulls licked clean

        Mortar of pasts crumble
unzipping my spine

        Dry lightning cracks as
blood spurts through the earth

        Burning my feet as it spills
        into the sun below me

Thick molten lead welds me to tarred soil

Primitive rhythms of bones banging by,
clattering femurs ancestral prize

    Dead of night shaking,
confrontations collide

        Jittery jaws blow out pent up sighs

        And I taste forgiveness
        as trapped breath releases

        The ripples expand
        until my image fades

    Life is generous while I am away

  I return to my smile and
meld with my skin,

  High noon in winter, and
dreamcast again

Sun Seduction

Carved oak bodies in lucid exhibitions

Silhouettes flickering in the Aries sun

Conversing with voracious curves

The sheen of orange alder over the swollen lake

The pines ravish the earth where I once walked

    And my lips tremble

    As I sear a black hole in the memory

Herbs upon her

She breathes of their scent

    Her dress houses the barrier of sounds

        Echoes in her delight

The tree trunk spreads its legs

    Exquisitely across the dirt

As it turns its face to shyly let a rock in between.

      A spider crawls up her web

        Tickling them both, alive

   What displays, so many artists here!

The roots bring water, the rock is stable

Holding life, but the rattlesnake hides

The king snake guards this piece of time, slithering through

Splendor wild of brave new hues, fragrant silky flowers

      The universe revealed alongside my toes, unafraid and

Fearless as pleasure's eyes spy

Supple skin oscillating with sultry epiphanies

           Prophesizing the moan of
      my moonstone tipped breast

An eruption from within

    In this rhythm of heat

The stream returns from its alder bark trip

Slowly refreshed, it drips and it drips

Gentle mist

    I unfold my legs like nature's way

    I dip my toes in saturated sand

Is it you again, the water from the tree?

        Where are you from, where are you going?

    The sun turns down his light

            Only a peek

Alongside imagination's coves I quiver

My naked thighs welcome the cool chill

Of the coming night

My feet gently pull from the tight sand

    And the chariot of the breeze

        Persuades me...

Night Stallions

The ground quakes, the horizon ripped in two

A line of the earth's crust splitting towards my feet

Moving monuments break from distant mountains, a wild stampede

The vibrating purple sky promises moonshine in the canter

Hidden in the hills

    Bare feet sprung high, stallions racing under my hips

    A transference of time

    Evocative gateway forbids my exit as I enter

    Majesties of manes tear through the silken night

Erotic souls enter peripheries

I clench dark tangles, twists and knots blown carefree by night

Mixed with my own light strands

    Streaks of strange lights streaming behind us

Smooth steed gliding and curing our blindness

    Rough as needed to break barricades

Arbiters of annihilation bucked away, stomping hurdles

        A rodeo of plucked petals flying everywhere

    The full moon thrusts into the sky

    Against the short solstice day

A full handover of luminescence to the longest nights

        The adornment of your jeweled black eyes

You are doorways anywhere, what colors my smile

    Transitory lover of sleep

Flung into faraway stars, the animal soul feels through me

        I am the mare

Galloping ardent hooves carry me past the hood of night

Kicking dusts of enchantment in our wake

                Distorting what ails us,
                  demolition of useless pasts

My reflection in constellations falls onto me like clothes

Naked in the grand elixir, transformed

       Independent of measure

Poured into waves of gyrating space

              Dissolved and

              Pulsing beyond the
          limits of form,

                  The tonic of
              tempering time

In the bed of forest in naked leaves

Moonbeams setting beyond heightened peaks

    One last trace

    Before she fades

        Close my eyes

        Staccato timed

            Heartbeats mine

            Dreamtime on

            Night stallion's ride

The Feminine Ignited

I've travelled through the stormy sense of evening

Awakened grace and curled up in white bear's hide

Where a chimney of sacred smoke's still piping

Inspired clouds come from the north fulfilling prophecies of ages

A purposeful revival

A temple goddess stands honored in the candlelight

Panting fire proclaims vowels of the feminine

The oldest language born from pure sky

Endless spans of hums transcend all limits

The chorus sings on high inside those walls

Made of trees that show
hints of their living stories

They tell of metals and planets
crafting symbols

Windy reeds they make of them at night

Where copper chimes and
bells ring time

To guide all who hear them

And poles of alder spell out
woman's story

Character lines shine in shapes of yonis

Real beauty lies inside their olden faces

Wisdom for the future of youths

The crystal paths that link
our inner destinies

Lattices that ink lines of self
into cohesive wholes

A soft structure to hold
strong our wild abandon

The ultimate trust of self

During every phase of woman

    Together held by the earth
as one in our waters

    Air breathes with fire

    Instinct over mind

As she reminds me of what we are

    Lotuses on river beds run by

I drift into chants of ancient goddesses

    Truth from every single spread of
the world

    And every interpretation of
the word

And my tendency turns toward the face of happiness

I send it to all women everywhere

First to those with the worst, then the least and the very most

    And us fortunate in between will
help carry it

I take it in and shred it into healing,
whatever it takes

It feels so right as flutes and strings
soothe me to sleep

I breathe bliss

And ladies dancing everywhere,
gold breasts and pink and black ones,

Burnt siennas and shimmery coppers,
natural as mud

We all play free, ecstatic and
laughing

Loving

A mandala of dream

And from every direction, the world
screams

Let it be her!

The feminine ignited.

Clarity

Slivers of rigid visions lighten, loosened

They froth into one, sights scrubbed clean and sharpened

Particles of wisdom catch as they blow by, before unnoticed

Scopes of panoramas encompass highs and lows

    The feeling of center

    The middle way walks us to clarity

Perspective uplifted from nothingness, outside of gravitational pulls

The distractive block of everything sidestepped

    Images form spontaneously through our own substance

The surfaces glossed with larger truth

    The choice of higher frequency

It is time for us to see, as people

The spirit guides and the lack of lines

> Ferried by sages, pillows stuffed with dreams

Mugwort which aids the intuitive woman

Fit here with talons and claws, speedy feet

Skin patched with leathers of resilient beasts

Every texture of feathered wings

> That move through all of space, beyond time, past all worlds and world ages

The intricate lace of our individual linings, unique, exquisite

> A creature all our own

>> We build it and feed it, draw details as we go

We can starve away or elevate the hate

> Telling love when to be gone or to go on and come visit

We fill up our pages that tell how we are
> So alone

And yet every one of us breathes of trees
> and feeds and

> is fed by the cycles of life

Moved by moods

Shaped by the senders of signs
> We can see if we can see, more helpful if we feel

> The late night gibbous moon, my carriage into morning

> A cold glint of time hits me fast with a silvered light

Slapped awake

Quiet mind
> An echo booms of everything that burned away,

> One last singe of haunted spirits dying.

Then the oak unveils the morning of the forest

Pink sun calls free the blackened mountains

> The freshened dew of dawn kisses my earthen flesh
>
> The magic smell of lavender induces me

To the mystic truth of early morning light, I'm listening

And the fading starry blanket of the brightening sky

> Answers glistening and
>> Now I see it clearly

Space for a Breath

From the sink of our throats our voices may speak

The bellowed crests of our lungs, aerated by practice

Conception at the collarbone

Sound and breath rhythmically pulse like lovers

My warrioress shoulders widen

The blades on my back bleed out wings

Bright golden wings, a friend of darkness

They hold hands behind us in private

Like lovers

The twinkle of stardust wipes clean my eyes

Allowing me to witness something wider

Tight chest wrought free

       Set traps snapped open,
       illusions dissolved

Sensations blink on lights at dusk

Breath grows roses around my heart

       Vining breadths of space
       between each bone

On wings of yogis, flown from the graves

Paths to truth wait to lead our own ways

       Secret hollow behind the heart

A personal temple, a space to create

       Ourselves

           and the impressions

           of the world we invite

To decorate our one true sacred place

The only thing that is really ours,

       the liberation of who we are

       and from where we understand

The flexibility and humility and

       Strength to change

And listen,

           Always listen

The only attendant be your breath

Charm

At play in the mountain sanctuary

      The blue heron's omniscient eyes,
an oracle of what to follow

Heaven and earth suspend water, a misty
miasma of spirit that lures us

      Deep into the wilderness

Pebbles washed smooth by the stream
roll under our feet

The Great Heron springs from a stone as
we run up the creek

Jumping waterfalls patrolled by
dragonflies,

Bubbling wake whisked by cobalt wings

That stretch over the stream connecting
trees

Oak and alder interlace, the gateway of
western sky

      We sing the Great Heron song
      she is teaching

And then we stop

                She flies beyond,
her charm is done

The cool clouded blur of the dampened sun lets out the occasional ray

That bursts through leaf speckled frames of branches

                And for one warm minute my breasts are washed with a transient light

And spikes of sunbursts thrust into the daytime

This grand presence lingering

She opens the sun as she flies to her heights

           Keep this alive,

                This feathered encounter with the divine

We say, giving birth to a spell by words

      And together this is ours

The drapes of reminiscence fall away

Then for the first time I see you

    In the portal of a magic moment

        A destined charm I chose

           Beloved

One

The bell tolls new again

A spillway of inspiration, a corridor of new air

Auspicious arrival comes the season's first rain

Benevolent Jupiter prophesizes, love for all gods

Rows of popping colors spurt fruits and flowers

Groves of gardens and trees run races for miles

Our pulses heal with nature as Mother

The rooted life on earth is breathing again

A clear drink from serpentine waters

    We all eat, learn the riches of squashes

    And we could toss them and paint their rinds and play,

Saying, hey, each one of them is unique too

A cornucopia of beauty

Such abundance matched

And then we join

In a circle

Every type of soul you could ever imagine

is there promising

to jump into the prism of love

And as a complete spectrum of light

We will charge together through storms

And miracles that we sometimes miss

we will start to notice

and onward we shall embark

on a procession of magic.

   Release,

    We light the fire

   The generous exhale

  That lets the night go out in
   perfect harmony

    The smoke clears,
forgiven

    And we are one.

www.ingramcontent.com/pod-product-compliance
Lightning Source LLC
Chambersburg PA
CBHW020556030426
42337CB00013B/1118